CHUPACABRA A Collection of Fifty Poems

Author: Raymond Lee

Copyright © Raymond Lee (2024)

The right of Raymond Lee to be identified as author of this work has been asserted by the author in accordance with section 77 and 78 of the Copyright, Designs and Patents Act 1988.

First Published in 2024

ISBN 978−1−83538−449−7 (Paperback)
978−1−83538−450−3 (Hardback)
978−1−83538−451−0 (E−Book)

Cover Design and Book Layout by:
White Magic Studios
www.whitemagicstudios.co.uk

Published by:
Maple Publishers
Fairbourne Drive, Atterbury,
Milton Keynes,
MK10 9RG, UK
www.maplepublishers.com

A CIP catalogue record for this title is available from the British Library.

All rights reserved. No part of this book may be reproduced or translated by any form or by any means, electronic or mechanical, including photocopying, recording or by any information storage and retrieval system without written permission from the author.

The views expressed in this work are solely those of the author and do not necessarily reflect the views of the publisher, and the publisher hereby disclaims any responsibility for them.

CHUPACABRA
A Collection of Fifty Poems

Raymond Lee

MAPLE
PUBLISHERS

CONTENTS

1. The speed of light 6
2. Panspermia 8
3. Planet of the Primates 10
4. Neanderthals 12
5. Water on Mars 13
6. Hovercraft 14
7. England's worst kings and queens 15
8. Three Horses 17
9. The Seeds 19
10. Silver Birch 21
11. The Rafflesia 23
12. The Rubra 25
13. Busy Lizzy 26
14. Red Hot Pokers! 27
15. Maple leaves 28
16. Yellowhammer 29
17. Hummingbird 30
18. Lion on the loose 32

19. Mad Elephant 33

20. Chimpanzee 35

21. Scolopendra! 36

22. Bacteria 37

23. 369 38

24. Black Helicopter 39

25. Doppelgänger 40

26. Secret Societies 41

27. In the caves 43

28. Something's going on 45

29. Nessie and the flying saucers 47

30. Waiting for the Anunnaki 48

31. From Mars 50

32. Strange weather 52

33. Thunderbird 53

34. Lava 55

35. Quicksand 56

36. Vlad 58

37. Scorpio 60

38. Chupacabra 62

39. Octopuses!	63
40. Neon lights	65
41. Chasing UFOs	66
42. UAP	67
43. Alien bases	68
44. The Greys	69
45. Chrononauts	70
46. The Project Blue Book	71
47. Son of perdition	72
48. There is no God	73
49. It takes all sorts	74
50. A poet's ode	75

Raymond Lee

The speed of light

At over a hundred and eighty-six thousand miles a second,
and that's the speed of light,
can you believe in moving so fast
across a universe so vast?

There's nothing can travel as fast as that,
but it's still 4.22 light years
to get to the nearest star
this science is so bizarre.

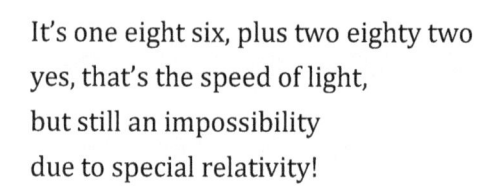

It's one eight six, plus two eighty two
yes, that's the speed of light,
but still an impossibility
due to special relativity!

And travelling at this incredible speed
an object's mass becomes infinite,
and so the energy to move it
we cannot even prove it.

At over a hundred and eighty six thousand miles a second
that is the speed of light,
can you believe in moving so fast
into the future, or back to the past?

And if we tried to go any faster
would there be a catastrophic reverse,
or a time and relative disaster,
an event horizon, or something worse?

Raymond Lee

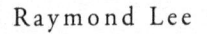

Panspermia

Could it be panspermia,
that brought life to our galaxy,
via space dust, comets, asteroids,
spacecraft and planetoids?

Was it just panspermia,
that swept the universe with seeds,
that drifted through the vastness of space,
and landed in a desolate place?

With bacteria and DNA embedded in rocks,
that then went interplanetary,
and took a journey into the void,
and so become an Anthropoid.

Or with radio panspermia
and a propagation in space,
it could be with radiation
that could also be the case.

Maybe a panspermia accident,
from a long, long time ago,
left by extra-terrestrial beings,
that then began to evolve and grow.

Could it be panspermia
the story of you and me,
and of all living creatures on this earth,
from stardust to a rebirth!

Raymond Lee

Planet of the Primates

On that third rock from the sun,
a planet in 'The Zone',
revolved a world of Hominids,
where Homo Sapiens made their home.

Where ape-like creatures like Gorillas
came down from the trees;
evolved into Neanderthals,
now bipeds walking with ease.

And so we didn't descend from Monkeys,
but from a line of Chimpanzee,
and from that same ancestor,
evolved quite differently.

Homo Sapiens and these cavemen
living alongside each other,
then natural selection came along,
and we took over from our brother.

but they're our exotic cousins,
and not just primitive brutes,
and I'm proud to be in their family
on this Earth, with my Simian roots!

Earth is the Planet of the Primates,
and we are the greatest of apes,
not evolved from a missing link,
just hairless Naked Apes!

Raymond Lee

Neanderthals

Now, you've never seen a Neanderthal,
but I'm sure you've met its cousin,
well there's a percent of its DNA,
in the human race today.

A hundred thousand years ago,
we met and mated them,
Neanderthals with human beings,
Hybrid women and men!

Neanderthals with their long, low skull,
with its ridge of a prominent brow,
Neanderthals and Homo Sapiens,
in the here and now.

Neanderthals and humans,
together in integration,
Neanderthals and human hybrids,
in our cities' population.

All hominids, all primates,
all searching for a truth,
for in Humans and Neanderthals,
in them we have the proof.

Water on Mars

Now there's water on Mars,
and what else will we find?
for the evidence is creeping closer to us
from clues that were left behind.

For underground are reservoirs
that lie deep within the surface,
and the water could fill the dry Martian oceans,
again the Red planet is stirring our emotions!

So is there life on Mars?
Now we've found it's water,
for on Earth that is where all life began,
then on to an evolutionary plan.

but are we being watched
by an intelligence, greater than ours,
from deep inside the planet's surface,
entities with deadly powers!

Raymond Lee

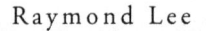

Hovercraft

Oh! How I loved the Hovercraft,
that rode on a cushion of air,
the invention to revolutionise,
travel everywhere.

It could move on land or sea,
and terrains of mud and ice,
swiftly too, from A to B,
this air cushion vehicle, ACV.

I remember a Hovercraft,
I went from Dover to Calais,
and the salty spray on that windy day,
that almost took my breath away!

What a great invention it was,
that had such great potential.....
An ocean liner coasting on air,
across the Atlantic to Delaware!

CHUPACABRA A Collection of Fifty Poems

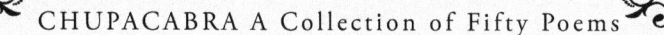

England's worst kings and queens

Now, open up your exercise books,
Mr Lewis, the teacher would say,
now this is a lesson, in the line of succession,
the worst sovereigns of the day!

There was the useless Mary, Queen of Scots,
the self-absorbed Edward the eighth
and the very brief reign of Lady Jane,
and George the third, who went insane!

And Richard the third and Henry the eighth,
all England's kings and queens
their Courtiers and their Reprobates,
causing scandalous scenes!

Now who was the most awful monarch of all?
It must be Henry the eighth!
That foul-tempered, bloodthirsty tyrant,
who broke away from the Catholic faith.

Fifty-seven thousand heads were removed,
during his reign of thirty-six years,
the 'Killer King' who took so many lives,
he beheaded them all, with two of his wives!

Raymond Lee

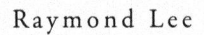

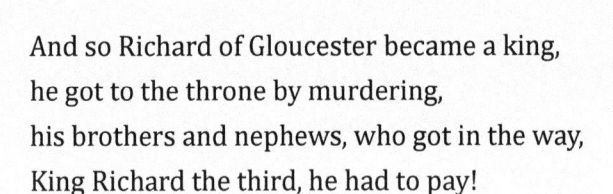

And so Richard of Gloucester became a king,
he got to the throne by murdering,
his brothers and nephews, who got in the way,
King Richard the third, he had to pay!

Henry of Richmond, he raised an army,
and killed Richard the third in battle,
and in Leicester he was found, in a car lot underground,
now old 'Crouchback's' bones won't rattle!

Now put down your exercise books,
for it's question and answer time,
how long did George the fourth reign?
And who was next in line!

I couldn't understand Mr Lewis's accent,
I thought maybe he was Welsh,
then I found it rather funny,
when I heard an almighty belch!

Mister Lewis collected the books,
for it was nearly four o'clock,
so that was the end of the lesson that day!
I stood up and laughed, and tore away!

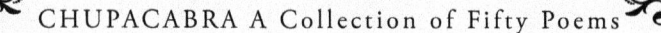

Three Horses

I watched the equines in the meadow,
a chestnut brown and dapple grey,
and saw a Piebald sleeping in the grass,
on this hot and sunny day.

Then I walked through a glade, and into trees,
and heard a gallop in the breeze,
three riderless horses were charging at me,
in fear and terror, I started to freeze.

The horse in the front had its eyeballs rolling,
for through the glade, I had just been strolling,
I decided to stand by the trunk of a tree,
and the horses cantered by.

For it was some labourers, I believe,
that were working on the perimeter fence,
that the horses jumped, and galloped away,
by breaking the paddocks' defence!

And so to the great Grand National Steeplechase,
in the spring of every year,
with its forty horses and riders or more,
and spectators and pundits that shout and roar!

I'd love to see them all finish the race,
without there being fallers,
clearing Foinaven fence and Becher's Brook,
from under starters' orders!

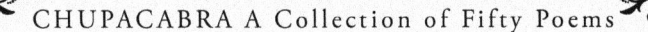

The Seeds

May I go to the shops dad,
and buy some seeds!
I want my own plot,
and get rid of those weeds.

To make my own choice
of whatever I fancy,
Wild flowers or Asters,
mixed seed or Pansy.

I purchased the seeds for him to see,
and he found a plot in the garden for me,
they germinated in a week,
for I was a ten-year old, gardening geek!

Then I used to mow the lawns,
the front garden then the back:
So fascinated by the mower blades' spin,.
and watching the grass drop into its bin.

I also planted a sunflower seed,
outside the sitting room window:
It must have grown seven feet tall,
the loftiest daisy of them all!

Raymond Lee

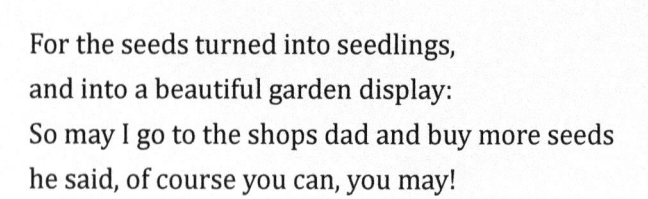

For the seeds turned into seedlings,
and into a beautiful garden display:
So may I go to the shops dad and buy more seeds
he said, of course you can, you may!

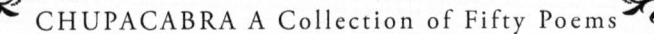

Silver Birch

I saw them in the summer on the way to the Lido,
an avenue of Silver Birches,
and saw them again on a country walk,
with a teacher and her nature talk.

I have seen Silver Birches in the forests,
and deep in the darkest wood,
in their silver trunks with their black diamond spots,
under their canopy I stood.

There were blue and long-tailed tits,
Redpolls and some Siskins,
Greenfinches and Nuthatches,
that fed upon their Catkins.

For it's where the Buff-tip moth will hide,
for it looks like a broken twig,
I saw one on its silver bark,
on a solitary specimen in a park.

The Woodpecker will even nest,
up in the older trees,
Deer and Hare will browse around,
through its twigs upon the ground.

Raymond Lee

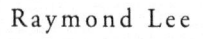

It's the awakening of a new life,
the Celtic tradition has said,
and so these are the words for the Silver Birch,
and now that you have read.

The Rafflesia

Have you seen that giant bloom,
that smells like rotting meat?
The Rafflesia from Indonesia,
so orange and so sweet!

For down its chalice sits a stool,
where on a plate, sit spikes,
and there's the sexual organs,
to procreate their types.

And so this smell of rotting flesh,
attracts the carrion flies,
then from male into the female,
with its viscous supplies.

Then seeds spread by the animals,
and insects will disperse,
and if a seed lands on a vine,
the cycle will traverse.

In Borneo and Sumatra,
on the vines that have dropped from the trees,
they start just like a cabbage,
wrapped in tightly closed-up leaves!

Raymond Lee

Then in the night the Rafflesia unfolds,
and behold its leathery petals,
in striking orange, with patches of cream,
it's a wonderful, botanical extreme!

And so behold the Bunga Padma,
the largest flower in the world,
and there sits that beautiful lotus,
with its brassy blooms unfurled.

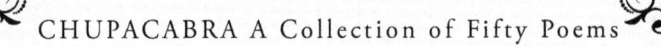

The Rubra

'Wow' it's like a Triffid,
it really is quite huge,
and this large Bromeliad,
she is wearing rouge!

This Brazilian 'Rubra',
so exotic and divine,
Maxima Imperialis,
with her chic design.

'Wow' it's like a Triffid,
so many, have said,
carnivorous it may not be,
but there's a flower spike of red!

So there it grows, the Rubra,
in this English garden now,
so tropical and bewitching,
it's a bombshell and a Wow!

Raymond Lee

Busy Lizzy

Busy Lizzy, touch me not,
shady lady grows a lot
over beds and borders, she
will hang in baskets, elegantly.

Busy Lizzy, Snapweed,
she of the exploding seeds
just sow them in a propagator and wait
for them all to germinate.

Her flowers are Zygomorphic
with a show of floral symmetry
for she will bloom for most of a year
such Busy Lizzy activity!

She dazzles in her Red and Pink
Violet and Coral too
in Yellow and White, that's oh so bright,
and even a shade of Lavender blue.

Blooming for you, right from the spring
until the frost starts biting
will grow for you at such a speed
this beautiful, exotic jewelweed.

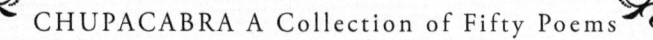

Red Hot Pokers!

They call them Red Hot Pokers,
for on their stems, are red hot blooms,
did they come straight out of a fire,
with their glorious, exotic plumes?

In blazing red, orange and yellow,
and on tapering flower heads,
the stunning Tritoma Torch lilies,
this Red Hot Poker spreads.....

Around an English country garden,
amongst all the floral delights;
There may stand majestically,
on stalks, these dazzling lights!

For there is The Royal Standard,
and the Royal Castle too,
standing regal and red, with their glowing spikes,
growing next to the Dahlias.... blue!

Raymond Lee

Maple leaves

In Red and Yellow, Orange and Gold,
hang the beautiful Maple leaves,
and there's syrup and wood, that's oh so good,
that come from the Maple trees.

And so the Maples bear the Samaras,
their wonderful flying seeds,
that spin around, 'til they touch the ground,
and sit among the weeds.

There's the Red Maple, Norway and Silver,
and many other varieties,
but the Sugar Maple is the best,
for it's far prettier than the rest!

And so the Maple's five lobed leaves,
adorn the branches in the breeze,
in Red and Gold, Orange and Yellow
hang Jewels and Gems, that look so mellow.

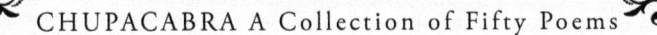

Yellowhammer

It sounds like 'a-little-bit-of-bread-and-no-cheese',
and so sings the yellowhammer in the trees,
a song 'with-a-little-bit-of-bread-and-no-cheese',
it's the yellow bunting, a-calling in the breeze.

Cock yellow bunting, sing a good song,
until the right hen bird comes along,
you must have a repertoire, large and true,
to be sure that she will come to you.

They may call you the 'scribble lark',
for all your eggs have scribble marks,
with lines and blotches, dashes and notches,
('tis why some call them the scribble larks).

Yellowhammer's bread and no cheese,
and so sings the yellow yorlin in the trees,
with its bright, canary yellow head,
'I've got no cheese, some seeds?' I said.

Emberiza Citrinella,
singing in a bush, that pretty yellow bird,
a bunting called a yellowhammer,
a bird 'tis seen and surely heard!

Raymond Lee

Hummingbird

Hummingbird, I felt your spirit,
hummingbird, I knew you were near,
oh hummingbird, you flying jewel,
from out of nowhere you seem to appear.

Oh hummingbird, sweet hummingbird,
was that my loved one close by?
then I saw you hovering near the bush,
the hum of your wings was your reply.

Then you hovered and stared at me,
so quizzically, so curiously,
was it to protect your territory,
and those flowers with nectar by the tree.

then you went flying backwards,
just like no other bird,
and behaving like a dragonfly,
that really was absurd!

But with its fiery coat of many colours,
gleaming from its neck and breast,
the fiery throated hummingbird,
surely is the very best.

Then hummingbirds were all around,
their colours flashing brightly,
and with pyrotechnics and of sound,
was a choral hum in harmony.

Raymond Lee

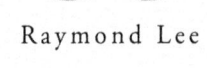

Lion on the loose

There's a Lion on the loose apparently,
What! A Lion on the loose?
Don't go out, there's a Lion about,
there's a Lion on the loose in Wembley!

There's a Lion on the loose in North London,
No! A Lion on the loose?
This is not a joke from a comical bloke,
a large cat....oh what a conundrum!

There's another one out in Surrey,
though I know all about that one,
the Surrey Puma was never caught,
and it's still out there on the run!

There's a Lion on the loose on the news,
I hope they don't come in twos,
so don't go out, there's a Lion about,
and don't put on your running shoes!

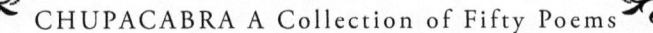

Mad Elephant

Its ears were flapping, its tail was flying,
then came a trumpeting display,
this Bull Elephant was very mad,
but I had a head start, and got away.

And so I took off across the field,
to find somewhere that I could shield.
Was I the only one to flee,
from this mad elephant running free?

Was this mammoth in my mind,
or from a fairground attraction, no longer confined!
Or did it come through a crack in time,
and I was the next in line!

The elephant was gaining ground,
with its screeching trumpeting sound,
and the stomping of its mighty feet.
as we ran along a street.

I did a deft left turn around a corner,
to escape its thunderous charge,
and it carried on running down the road,
a confused and mighty mammal at large.

But then it swung around, and back again,
and continued its chase after me,
now there's more people around to pursue,
I only wish it would chase them too!

And so I came out from a hiding place,
when I thought I had the all clear,
and the elephant, it was standing there,
just waiting for me to run somewhere.

And so once more, I ran again,
and it wasn't far behind,
for you can't outrun a bull elephant,
especially one out of its mind!.....

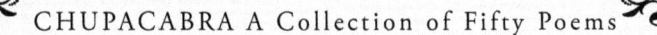

Chimpanzee

I find the Chimpanzee so scary,
when he grins and bares his teeth,
showing his sardonic smile,
an ape with cunning, strength and guile.

If one escaped and ran amok,
everyone would flee in shock,
it would have come from a circus or zoo,
or was it a pet that went crazy?!

Would you believe its DNA,
is much the same as ours,
but this Hominid is a beast,
a wild animal to say the least!

The Orangutan and Bonobos,
the Mountain and Lowland Gorilla too,
they're all a part of our family,
great apes, like me and you.

But this is about the Chimpanzee,
our closest relative,
so don't get too near, he might rip you apart
when he's an adult, intelligent and smart!

Raymond Lee

Scolopendra!

What is that!.....A Scolopendra?
a-scuttling down the hallway......
what on earth!... how did it get here?
The centipede from hell.

A Scolopendra Gigantea,
a giant Arthropod,
from northern south America,
this really is quite odd!

What shall I do, who should I call,
now it's running up the wall!
a pest controller I must find,
to deal with bugs, bugs of this kind.

A Scolopendra, what a shock!
now it's wound around my clock,
motionless, and lying in wait
menacingly, for some juicy bait!

But where did it come from, I don't know,
now it's putting on a show.
Are there more to come under the door,
to scamper across the carpeted floor?

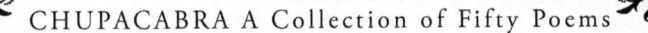

Bacteria

They reproduce, it's binary fission,
into doubles, that's their mission,
their daughters and their DNA,
consume nutrition on the way.

We're like bacteria, microscopic,
we're quantum physics on display,
just bacteria, single cells,
I'm looking at with some dismay.

Just reproducing, multiplying,
like bacterial growth,
and consuming all of the earth's resources,
like locusts, humans both.

We're like bacteria, endoscopic,
we're quantum physics on display,
just bacteria, single cells,
I'm looking at with such dismay.

Micro-organisms, good and bad,
and looking through this microscope,
I see the microbes multiply,
watching them with my prying eye!

Raymond Lee

369

Three six and nine,
are they numbers that point to a route divine?
three six and nine,
are these figures a clue or a sign?

What a strange anomaly,
with Tesla and his theory,
whatever you divide one by,
it's always three six nine but why?

Is it the Holy Trinity,
the three six nine divinity,
the Father, Son and the Holy Ghost,
numbers that we see the most.

Why do these figures all align,
is three six nine a code in time,
and is there a barcode in this mix?
and the devil with his bag of tricks!

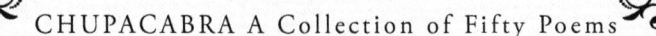

Black Helicopter

Hovering silently like a giant Bat
the Black Helicopter stared at me
I froze in fear, why is it here
What is this black shape I fear?

The Black Helicopter, darkened windows
who were the pilots? The Men in Black?
It wouldn't surprise me in the least,
are they preparing to attack?

Black Helicopter, out of nowhere
just appeared so menacingly,
Black Helicopter or fallen angel,
or a nightmare beckoning threateningly!

Raymond Lee

Doppelgänger

Another me? There cannot be!
what a strange anomaly:
My Doppelgänger in the crowd,
a copy of me, is this allowed?

My twin, my double, maybe trouble,
there could be a face off
for this town ain't big enough,
and a battle royal could be rough!

How dare there be a look-a-like,
such similarity,
but from the chaos in the universe,
can come familiarity!

I don't mind having a striking resemblance,
to a person I'll never know,
for they haven't seen me, or have I them,
until we make a show.

Until then, there's a double walker,
a shadow of myself,
but should I meet my Doppelgänger,
and what about yourself?

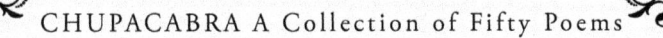

Secret Societies

All you have to do is ask,
to get a consultation
to join this warrior band of men,
and be part of a syndication.

With the square and the compasses,
and the eye of providence,
the Freemasons and their sign,
protecting the grand design.

There were warriors that guarded the Christian pilgrims,
making their way to the holy land,
The Knights Templar of Temple Mount,
the poor fellow soldiers of Christ.

Jesus didn't die on the cross,
and did not ascend to heaven,
but went to a monastery in Carmel,
is what the Rosicrucians tell!

And the Bavarian illuminati
and their enlightenment through reason,
and the Jesuits, Kabbalah,
inspiring their cohesion.

Raymond Lee

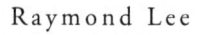

The order of the Skull and Bones,
the building called The Tomb,
at Yale the seniors are tapped,
for a meeting in that windowless room!

And so at Bilderberg, Bill Clinton,
and Margaret Thatcher too,
there was Angela Merkel and Tony Blair,
and the Chatham House rule they knew.

Then mystery and conspiracy,
and banners in the streets,
saying 'Stop this new world order',
amongst the chaos and disorder!

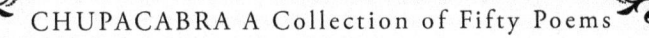

In the caves

Through caves and caverns,
Grottos and hollows,
with flint by fossils,
sinews and bone,
are labyrinths of mystery,
weaving a maze of history.

Through honeycombs of darkness,
to catacombs of gloom,
there's a roadway to a secret tomb,
in a gallery of ancient times,
turnings and alleys with mythical signs.

There's Anglo Saxons and Troglodytes,
Dolerites in Stalactites,
a Druids' sacrificial play,
centuries pass along the way!

Hidden chambers, sunken vaults,
with treasures from a far- off land,
a rogues' and villains' hideaway,
the smugglers in a Cornish bay.

Raymond Lee

Black cloaked, awesome figures,
go filing through the passageways,
their flaming torches burning bright,
these monks are chanting their holy rite.

Witches on a full moon,
and wizards, both conspiring doom,
consult the heavens, and curse the brave
mortals, who venture into their cave.

In caves and caverns,
with their grottos and shrines,
there's romance and magic,
in those Hollows and mines,
and in all those weird and mysterious spaces
in the caves, those ancient places!

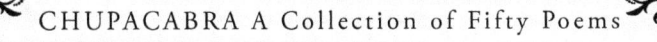

Something's going on

The aliens are getting closer,
the entities are drawing near,
and foreign objects in the sky,
something's going on up there!

There's a misinformation campaign,
to try and drive us all insane,
a cover up on a global scale,
but will the governments explain!

There's something going on up there,
and it's not the Russians or Chinese,
there's a fleet of UFOs flying around,
at many times faster than the speed of sound!

And hovering around the storage areas,
at every nuclear military base,
to learn of our technology,
before they show their face!

There's something happening all around us,
have you seen them too?
and witnesses told to shut their mouths,
or they'll get what they are due!

Raymond Lee

Is the pentagon using the military,
as experimental guinea pigs,
and have the beings from another planet,
found another world to inhabit?

People afraid to speak out or come forward,
for they know not what to expect,
and there's spaceships coming from out of the clouds,
extraterrestrial, i suspect!

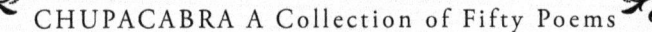

Nessie and the flying saucers

Nessie and the flying saucers,
Sasquatch and the missing link,
the aliens are the men in black,
the dinosaurs are not extinct!

Nessie and the flying saucers,
in the Fortean Times,
with crop circles in the county of Wiltshire,
and Alfred Watkins Ley lines.

Nessie and the flying saucers,
all under strange phenomena,
and in the flying saucer review,
encounters of the third kind too!

Nessie and the flying saucers,
the landing at Socorro,
the Mothman of Point Pleasant,
he could return tomorrow.

It's just Nessie and the flying saucers,
Nessie and the rest,
with unidentified flying objects,
and a Pterodactyl's nest!

Raymond Lee

Waiting for the Anunnaki

I'm just waiting for a visitation,
in their mighty craft,
the watchers with their ray guns,
the Anunnaki from the past.

For they may have built the pyramids,
and other structures too,
those ancient astronauts from far away,
may soon return with a lights display!

Just waiting for the Reptoids,
from the planet Nibiru,
anticipating their arrival,
with a mighty crew.

I'm waiting for the Anunnaki,
waiting for the day,
when the gods of the Sumerians,
will come and have their say.

Hail! The Anunnaki,
Hail! Majestic gods,
save us from extermination,
by Lucifer's lightning rods!

The Anunnaki are in their spaceship,
the Anunnaki are on their way,
and if it's not for gold this time, or slaves,
what else I pray?

Raymond Lee

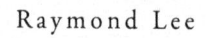

From Mars

Do you believe we came from Mars?
were our origins from the stars,
are we from the red planet,
that once we did inhabit?

Did you believe in the little green men?
from a hundred years ago, and then,
we changed our outlook, learnt something new
about the Martian point of view.

Did microbes come from Mars to Earth,
and one day to return there,
not a strange place anymore,
but fully terraformed to the core!

Came from Mars, Phobos and Deimos,
to this world to pro-create,
life forms from earth, to Mars and back,
and forth again to propagate!

They came from Mars to be reborn,
for we're beings from another world,
from cosmic dust to insectoids,
and then to Martian humanoids!

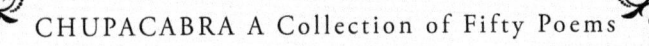

Now, do you believe we came from Mars?
how strange that seems to be,
but we must be the Martians surely,
the truth about you and me!

Raymond Lee

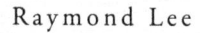

Strange weather

I saw a white feather floating down,
was this an omen from the sky?
Is it now a world at the end of its tether,
and the reason for this strange weather?

For now the winter is spring, and autumn is summer,
no snow is forecast, and the winter's now past,
and places feel strange with this climate change,
now this blanket of grey that depresses this day.

Humidity is what used to be,
in ice and snow.. now wintry,
have the seasons crossed their boundary?
Are we near the end of time!

All I can hear is silence now,
but for the sound of a strange and constant hum,
what is coming, what's on its way,
along with this strange weather today!

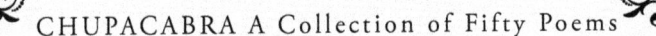

Thunderbird

Once I saw a cryptid bird,
and heard its terrible cries,
the legend that is the Thunderbird,
with the lightning from its eyes.

I read a thunderbird flew over Pennsylvania,
and a Pterodactyl was seen in Tombstone,
and a giant bird in Illinois,
that almost carried off a boy.

The Thunderbird, said Nanabozho,
he conquers the upper world,
he rules over the serpent and his horns,
for they are mighty Teratorns.

And he who sees the Thunderbird,
during its solitary feast,
will be a war chief for his people,
a warrior, a powerful beast!

And so the Thunderbird defended the Sioux,
from the Dakota Serpent,
this powerful spirit had magnificent wings,
a giant bird that did magical things……

Raymond Lee

And so I heard a whoosh of wings behind me,
and thunder in the air,
I turned around in terror,
then hid, and said a prayer,
then I turned around to see it again, but the Thunderbird wasn't there!

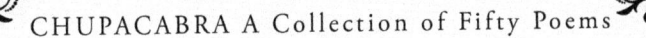

Lava

I'm watching the lava moving slowly,
the lava creepily flows,
the lava is coming straight towards me,
like something from a horror show!

White hot lava streams are crawling,
down the mountainside,
was this like earth at the very beginning,
or did two worlds collide?

And then bright orange, a glowing red,
then brown and into black,
that molten rock becomes the lava,
it is now on the attack!

I can see another eruption,
a volcanic disturbance for sure,
another explosion from the side of the mountain,
more magma, then lava galore!

And another explosion that's too much to bear,
I had to escape, get away from there,
for it was just an adventure, a scary dream,
a nightmare with a piercing scream!

Raymond Lee

Quicksand

Don't fall into the quicksand,
be careful where you tread,
the ground below may look well-trodden,
but there may be danger ahead.

Just beware of the quicksand,
for it'll take you by surprise,
it will trap you, then will suck you down,
before you realise!

You'll become hysterical,
you're now caught in a trap,
in its snare, caught unaware,
in its silt and water lair.

If you step on to quicksand,
you may disturb a beast,
but there may be a warning sign,
a danger sign at least.

If you get stuck in that quagmire
let the sand and water flow,
move a little, loosen its grip,
you'll only sink to waist and hip.

It could be perilous by the coast though,
with that hazard, that compound,
so shout for help and rescuers,
to help you onto solid ground.

Raymond Lee

Vlad

So brutal and cruel was Vlad the impaler,
he staked on poles, twenty thousand men,
others were skinned and buried alive,
roasted and hacked, and repeated again!

Brutal and cruel was Vlad the impaler,
a commander and a ruler too,
there was Mercea the elder, then Stephen the great,
now Vlad the third, with so much hate!

The Turks had held him captive,
for he was just a young prince, a hostage,
with a hatred for the Ottoman empire,
that festered and it grew.

His brother Radu, the handsome,
he chose the side of the Turks,
now Vlad the third had been betrayed,
he then went on a bloody crusade.

The mighty Ottoman empire,
was halted in its tracks,
Wallachia and Transylvania,
defended from its attacks!

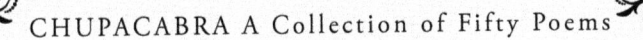

But Vlad, his head was decapitated,
and sent to Sultan Mehmet II,
and in Constantinople there's a a trophy,
for all the Turks to see!

Vlad Dracula was his other name,
for this story, it is true,
and he even drank the blood of virgins,
and was the devil incarnate too!

Raymond Lee

Scorpio

With dark angels and spirits, grotesque and macabre,
he's part of a secret society,
the supernatural and the occult,
this scorpion scuttles around in the vault!

With underworld connections,
this Scorpio's in a film noir,
he's hard to handle, and ready to strike,
he's lying in wait, 'til the time is right!

Running into danger without a second thought,
this Scorpion is brave, situation fraught!
he is secretive, jealous, ambitious, demanding,
his mind's probing power is ever commanding.

He's a little bit psychic, and psychotic too,
with a powerful presence, and a tough-minded view
and a penchant for mystery, it's an interesting sign,
if you deflate his ego, be gentle and kind.

Not fazed by others' opinions of him,
he is misunderstood, he is harsh and is grim,
there's no sting in the tail of this story, but I know,
about the story of Scorpio.

It was a giant Scorpion that killed Orion,
and all through jealousy,
Orion boasted he could kill any beast,
but it was Apollo who killed he!

Raymond Lee

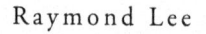

Chupacabra

Have you heard of the Chupacabra,
the spikey- backed blood sucking beast?
It all started in Puerto Rico
where the cryptid loved to feast!

First it was a reptilian biped,
the 'Goatsucker' was it's name,
it sucked the blood of goats and sheep,
then a legend it became!

Was it a giant vampire bat,
or experimental hybrid rat,
with Sasquatch too, and all of that,
now a Chupacabra jumps out of that hat!

Have you seen the Chupacabra?
Could it be a hairless dog,
a rabid Coyote devil,
or a Canis Lupus mog?

Do you believe in the Chupacabras,
seen a spiky-backed blood sucking beast?
Maybe it's just a mad mutt on the loose,
or it's paranormal at the least!

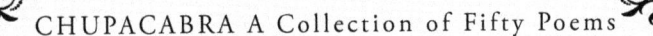

Octopuses!

What are those writhing blobs,
that go sweeping through our oceans?
With their eight arms, those tentacles,
with bulbous heads and ventricles!

With three hearts and nine brains
and blue blood in their veins,
they're new kings of the ocean,
in Cephalopod motion.

An octopus can open jars,
and find its way out of a maze,
then squeeze into a tiny space,
they really are a weird case!

When changing colour, changing shape,
for prey and hunted, there's no escape,
will it be the same for us
this is something to discuss!

For they'll come out of the water,
and scrabble over the rocks,
they've been seen in many places,
and even around the docks.

Raymond Lee

Are they just large molluscs,
that have escaped from their shell,
on the loose, and still evolving,
creatures from a nightmare hell?

So where did the octopus come from?
With the Nautilus and the squid,
did it come from stardust,
with its DNA and plasmid?

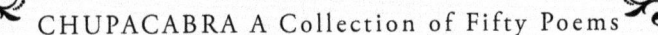

Neon lights

For some down town jazz,
by a theatre queue,
for something exotic,
and a game for two,

I just love those plasma signs,
like neon lights, amid the city sights.

There were installations in Times square,
and in Las Vegas, and everywhere,
now it's LED and plasma screens,
that lure us to our lurid dreams.

There's neon lights to seedy bars,
and red lights in the red quarter,
it's twilight time in metropolis,
it stands waiting for the populace.

And I just love its plasma lights,
like neon signs, amid city sights.

Just waiting for the lights to change,
I'm at a junction, something strange,
a glowing object in the sky,
and is that a star that's shooting by?

Raymond Lee

Chasing UFOs

Was I just chasing UFOs,
or just searching for the truth,
about life and death and the paranormal,
now remembering my youth?

I gazed in awe at a rainbow,
and never stared into the sun!
looked up into the night-time sky,
and watched the stars, and gave a sigh.

Was I just chasing UFOs,
that then just disappeared,
and still believed in a higher power,
or something very weird?

For I'm still chasing mysterious lights,
still looking for wondrous signs,
and get so excited at mysterious glows
forever chasing UFOs.

UAP

It's a phenomenon we all know,
that used to be a UFO,
was unidentified in the sky,
unknown objects that could fly.

Flying saucers, flying discs,
and cigar shaped with some portals,
and some triangular and in formation,
some exuding radiation.

It's UAPs that now we see,
and with this simple acronym,
name unidentified aerial things,
that hover, then shoot off without wings!

Raymond Lee

Alien bases

Are you still searching, looking up,
still gazing into the sky?
for the alien bases are now underground,
that's where the UFOs are to be found.

And look out to the oceans and the seas,
for those enigmatic UAPs,
and watch them dive from outer space,
to hide in a secret watery place.

They are way up in the Arctic,
way down in Antarctic too,
the aliens in their spacecraft,
hide in places, hard to pursue.

For they're out there deep in the jungle,
and there in the desert dunes,
and hiding in the deepest parts of the earth,
enclosed in their cocoons.

And when the time is ready to reveal themselves,
us humans will all stand aghast,
as they all come out of their tunnels and caves,
with their plans, and nets to cast!

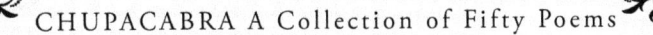

The Greys

They'll come through the ceilings,
they'll come through the walls,
come up from the floors,
to place their spores,
they'll enter your body,
and enter your mind,
put a chip in your head,
and leave it behind!

The Greys are coming,
they don't open doors,
they'll just appear at your bed,
the Greys are coming, and no one is safe,
for they're just like the walking dead.

The Greys will enter your inner sanctum,
and violate your outer skin,
experiment and torture,
and place a wire within,
for they'll come through their very own portal,
to enter our dimension,
the Greys are here I fear,
and what is their intention?

Raymond Lee

Chrononauts

Can you feel their presence,
or sense an ominous threat?
Are entities slipping down a wormhole of time,
or through the internet?

Are they inter-dimensional,
or just from outer space,
maybe time travellers from our future,
on a mission, on a case.

Greys or Hybrids staring down,
you'll be lying on a rack,
it's an abduction, then a visitation,
from the men in black!

But don't let the reptilians get you,
avoid them at all cost,
for they're just evil extra-terrestrials,
just looking for the lost.

They're all time-travellers, Chrononauts,
travelling through other dimensions,
on a time loop, a space-time curve,
in their time travelling inventions.

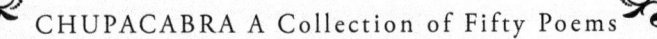

The Project Blue Book

They were all put into the project blue book,
those cases on the UFOs,
were they a threat to our national security?
What were those objects, heaven knows!

They were all put in the project blue book,
to study and analyse,
anything out of the ordinary,
and peculiar that flies!

All that aerial phenomena,
that couldn't be explained,
they were all filed away to study,
in Wright-Patterson they remained.

And so the project blue book,
for all its seventeen years,
investigated and summarised,
to dispel the public's fears.

For there was no security threat,
or strange extra-terrestrial vehicles,
but an unexplained twenty-three per cent,
and so the project blue book came and went!

Raymond Lee

Son of perdition

This man, the son of perdition,
'tis a man, yet not a man,
but a vile and grotesque entity,
'tis Satan's evil progeny.

The spawn of the serpent and the beast,
he'll be the lawless one,
and with his loathsome countenance,
behold the devil's son!

With a bulbous head, Medusa's hair,
a hump in his back, and a green-eyed stare,
a stomping gait, a complexion pale,
It's Lucifer's son, on Earth somewhere.

This thing, sent from the pit of hell,
the anti-Christ, oh can't you tell,
he's a deceiver, he'll fool everyone,
declare he is god, he will claim he's the one.

This man, the son of perdition,
a man, yet not a man,
will be destroyed in the lake of fire,
according to god's plan.

There is no God

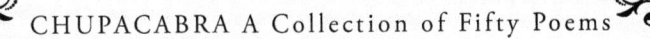

There is no God, no alien beings,
as far as I can see,
and no afterlife, no rebirth,
just a lonely destiny.

Just a world that's turning in space,
on the edge of our galaxy,
can anything hear us, do they fear us?
for we may not have any company!

How big is the universe,
are we really all alone?
Was this world just one big fluke,
now a planet that we call home?

Where is God and his angels,
that we have yearned to see?
are they travelling at the speed of light,
to meet us in eternity?

Raymond Lee

It takes all sorts

It takes all sorts of people.
with their foibles and their ways,
to make a world that's different,
not just dull shades and greys.

It takes all races and their creeds,
being fruitful, sowing seeds,
to stir a melting pot, a potion,
on a planet in constant motion.

It takes all sorts to make a world,
with all their idiosyncrasies,
let's embrace, not push away,
make harmonies and symphonies.

But it only takes two people,
and this line where there's a Turtle dove,
it takes all sorts to make a world,
and two to fall in love.

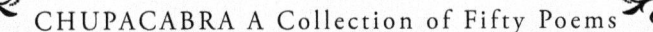

A poet's ode

I am a poet,
and now you know it,
a poet in this town,
I am a poet, a Bard I be,
a poet of renown!

William Wordsworth,
Shelley and Lee,
they've got nothing at all on me,
when I'm writing prose right out of my tree,
with a sonnet and a soliloquy!

I am a poet,
yes now you know it,
'cause I've just swallowed a dictionary,
I'm a sonneteer and balladeer,
but nothing rudimentary!

This is poetry,
and here's a bit more,
I'm a poet with a capital P,
a Rhymester and a Troubadour,
for this poem has created me!